The GOLDEN AGE of SAIL

AMY HANDY

TODTRI

ACKNOWLEDGMENTS

The golden age of sail is a subject so extensive and so rich in fascinating detail that the greatest challenge in writing this book was condensing a wealth of material into a more manageable scope. Researching the illustrative material presented the same difficulty; there are so many wonderful visuals to accompany this theme that the prospect of making choices at times seemed overwhelming.
I am grateful to Douglas Handy, Information Services Developer at Mystic Seaport, Mystic, Connecticut, for his initial help in approaching the topic; how fortunate that someone so involved in this subject also happens to be my brother-in-law. Thanks also go to Nathan R. Lipfert, librarian at the Maine Maritime Museum, Bath; and to Jean Perla, for serving as navigator on my voyage to that museum. I am especially grateful to Cynthia Sternau of Todtri Productions, an editor for whom I have tremendous respect and with whom I always enjoy working.
Finally, I would like to thank Christopher Handy, not only for his emotional support, but for his military research contribution and his knowledgeable evaluation of the manuscript. And thanks, too, to Julia Handy, for her patient understanding that having a mom who works at home often means having to share her with a time-consuming project.

This book was designed and produced by Todtri Productions Limited P.O. Box 572, New York, NY 10116-0572 FAX: (212) 279-1241

Printed and bound in Singapore

ISBN 1-880908-89-1

Author: Amy Handy

Publisher: Robert M. Tod
Editorial Director: Elizabeth Loonan
Designer and Art Director: Ron Pickless
Production Coordinator: Heather Weigel
Senior Editor: Edward Douglas
Project Editor: Cynthia Sternau
Associate Editor: Shawna Kimber
Picture Researchers: Julie Dewitt, Natalie Goldstein,
    Kate Lewin, Cathy Stastny
Research Assistant: Laura Wyss
Typeset and DTP: Blanc Verso/UK

PICTURE CREDITS

Art Resource, New York pp. 21, 46, 64 (bottom)

Bridgeman/Art Resource pp. 42 (bottom), 66 (top)

The Bridgeman Art Library pp. 4, 6–7, 8–9, 10, 11, 12 (top), 13, 14 (top & bottom), 16–17, 20 (bottom), 29, 30–31, 32 (top & bottom), 33, 34, 36, 41, 43, 44 (bottom), 48, 52, 56, 59, 65, 67, 76 (top)

Esto Photographics pp. 8 (left), 9 (right), 24 (bottom), 54 (top & bottom)

Mary Evans Picture Library pp. 5, 20 (top), 23, 28 (bottom), 35, 37, 38 (top & bottom), 39, 40, 45 (left & right), 49, 50–51, 62, 77 (top)

Giraudon/Art Resource p. 12 (bottom)

Erich Lessing/Art Resource pp. 60–61

The Mariners' Museum, Newport News, Virginia p. 76 (bottom)

Mirror Syndication International pp. 25, 26, 63

National Museum of American Art, Washington, D.C./Art Resource pp. 74–75

Nawrocki Stock Photo pp. 19 (top), 55, 66 (bottom), 77 (bottom)

North Wind Picture Archive pp. 28 (center), 64 (top), 68 (top & bottom), 69, 70–71, 72 (top & bottom), 73

Picture Perfect pp. 15, 18, 22

P&O Steam Navigation Company p. 27

Scala/Art Resource p. 47

South Street Seaport Museum, New York pp. 19 (bottom), 24 (top), 28 (top), 42 (top), 44 (top), 53 (top & bottom), 57

Lois Wagner pp. 58, 78–79

CONTENTS

INTRODUCTION 4

Chapter One
THE MAGIC OF SAIL 10

Chapter Two
THE SEAFARING LIFE 34

Chapter Three
THE ROMANCE AND
TERROR OF THE SEA 56

INDEX 80

ℐNTRODUCTION

Opposite: His name virtually synonymous with *pirate,* Blackbeard excelled at the pirate stratagem of causing utmost terror in his victims. From his huge black beard and smoldering hat to his brace of pistols and daggers, he was a formidable opponent indeed.

THE TALL SHIPS
AND THEIR FORERUNNERS

A's for the anchor that swings at our bow,
B's for the bowsprit through the wild seas do plough.
C's for the capstan we merrily around,
D are the davits we lower our boats down.
Now E for the ensign that flies at our peak,
F is for the fo'c's'le where the good sailors sleep.
G for the galley where the cooks hop around,
H are the halyards we haul up and down.
I's for the irons where our booms ship,
J's for the jibs that so neatly do sit.
K's for the keelson, of which we are told,
L's for the lanyard that keeps a good hold.
Now M is the mainmast so neat and so strong,
N for the needle that never points wrong.
O for the oars we row our boats out,
P for the pumps that will keep her afloat.
Q for the quarterdeck, where our officers stand,
R for the rudder, keeps the ship in command.
S for the sailors, who move her along,
T for the topsails we hoist with a song.
U for the Union which flies at our peak,
V for the victuals which the sailors do eat.
W for the wheel where we all take our turn,
X, Y, Z is the name on our stern.
     —"The Sailor's Alphabet"

Above: Four members of the French Navy man a cannon during the Napoleonic Wars. The man in the black hat holds a pair of calipers, used to measure the vertical angle of the cannon for a more accurate shot.

For more than two and a half centuries, the great sailing ships ruled the waves, and the nations with the most powerful vessels ruled the world. In an era when a simple journey between cities was an arduous trek by horse and carriage, long before trains or automobiles, when flying was no more than a dream, ships provided the swiftest means of reaching far-off destinations and exploring new worlds.

Ships offered windows onto the globe. Undiscovered continents could be mapped and unknown seas charted. Products from home could be traded and sold, and novel goods from exotic lands brought back for the domestic market. And war could be waged, more efficiently and more decisively than ever before. The countries that conquered the seas gained supreme political authority and ensured their own economic prosperity.

The creation of the boat was as important as the invention of the wheel.

Right: With only two square-rigged masts and fore-and-aft rigging on the mizzen, the *Molly* is technically not a ship; this type of vessel is known as a bark.

Above: Sailors generally lived hard lives and earned little money, but captains frequently lived quite well, as evidenced by this Massachusetts sea captain of the 1830s posing in expensive clothes.

For thousands of years, people have sought to improve transportation by water, developing ever more sophisticated materials and designs to make traveling safer, easier, and faster. The very first boat was probably a simple floating log, then perhaps a bundle of lashed-together reeds, until someone thought to carve out the log to create a hollow shell that would not only float but would provide some manner of seating. These craft were at first propelled by hand or paddle.

Then came the sail. Evidently some clever person realized that by stringing up a piece of cloth on a pole stuck in the middle of the boat, the wind could help do some of the work in powering the craft. The earliest known picture of a sail, from the Nile Valley in Egypt, is almost eight thousand years old. The four-sided sail that it depicts came to be known as a square sail, not for its shape (square sails are not necessarily square and in fact are often trapezoidal) but because the pole from which it hangs (known as the yard) crosses the mast at a right angle. The ancient Egyptians, Greeks, Phoenicians, and Romans all used square sails, as did the Vikings, and the Northern Europeans during the middle ages. But many

Left: A British ship, said to be the *Dutton,* looms moments away from shipwreck. The vessel may have been "pooped," meaning that a wave has broken over the stern, which can set the ship drastically off course.

Below: National leaders were a popular subject for figureheads. This likeness of Ulysses S. Grant, dating from about 1865–75, sports over twenty coats of paint, since the damage wrought by wind and sea often necessitated annual repainting.

centuries passed before seagoing vessels relied entirely on the power of the wind; for a long time they depended on a combination of sails and oars. When Greece and Rome sought to expand their empires, they utilized the galley or the trireme, outfitted with a sail or two and as many as eighteen hundred slaves or prisoners to serve as oarsmen, ranged in three levels. The Viking longboat—feared throughout Europe in the dark ages—needed a row of oarsmen along each side to supplement its single sail.

Eventually, ships powered entirely by sail replaced galleys. Relying on a very large crew to man the oars, the galley's range was limited by its necessity to restock supplies frequently. In addition, its wide-open hull and narrow bow rode low on the water, making it ill suited to a long voyage on the open sea. Though the galley endured until the late 1700s, the sailing ship's stronger composition and roomier accommodation enabled more far-reaching voyages and made for easier handling in rough weather. By the 1700s, sailing ships had evolved into swift and powerful floating fortresses. They were to reign supreme until the introduction of steam propulsion in the mid-nineteenth century.

$\mathcal{T}$HE MAGIC OF SAIL

It's oft I've seen that gallant ship with the wind abaft her beam,
With her royals and her stunsails set, a sight for to be seen,
With the curling wave from her clipper bow a sailor's joy to fell,
And the canvas taut in the whistling breeze logging fourteen off the reel.

—"The *Flying Cloud*"

$\mathcal{H}$umans have taken to the water for thousands of years, to fish or to trade, to fight or to explore. From the simple, early attempts at water travel, floating craft gradually evolved into a highly sophisticated arrangement of sails and rigging atop an ever-changing silhouette built for battle, to discover new worlds, or to ferry cargo to ports around the globe.

SHIP DESIGN

Throughout the age of sail, ship design sustained a number of transformations that changed silhouettes and influenced sailing characteristics. By the eighteenth century, with the major powers of Europe vying for domination of the seas, ships were essentially floating fortresses. As design was simplified, the number of different types of vessels decreased. In the late 1600s there were five classes of vessels with twenty-four different gun arrangements; by 1786 there were only three types remaining, with generally uniform gunnery organization. Ships generally engaged in battle single file to maximize the effect of the multiple gun decks. The length of a warship was determined by the number of guns on each deck. The number of guns in turn determined the rate of the ship. In Britain, a first-rate ship carried over a hundred cannon. The mainstay of

Opposite: The seventy-gun ship of the line *Resolution* rides out a gale. Heavily armed vessels such as this were used by England during the seventeenth century in their battle with Holland for mercantile dominion.

Below: Sailors have always had a reputation for uncivilized behavior. In *Ship with Armed Men*, sixteenth-century artist Hans Holbein portrays the crew with more than a hint of satire: liquor is passed around and consumed freely; one sailor vomits over the side; another carouses with a prostitute.

Right: Built in 1637, the *Sovereign of the Seas* was the first three-deck warship ever crafted. By the eighteenth century, with all the major powers of Europe competing for maritime supremacy, ships had essentially become floating fortresses.

Below: The elaborately carved and gilded ornamentation once favored on ships—as seen here in a seventeenth-century Dutch painting—later gave way to simpler painted decoration.

the British and French battlefleets in the late eighteenth and early nineteenth centuries was the seventy-four-gun third-rater. The largest ships in the young American navy of the time were forty-four-gun frigates.

Seventeenth-century steering gear was located outside the hull. The tiller, fixed to the top of the rudder, came through a rectangular opening large enough to permit wide lateral movement in steering. Because this design

Above: Taken from a Robert Burns poem about witches, the name *Cutty Sark* is a Scottish term meaning "short shirt." Many ships have unusual appellations, but this may be one of the strangest of all.

reconnaissance and for fending off pirates. By 1785 the British fleet contained nearly as mainly frigates as ships of the line. French frigates proved quite adept during the wars of the Empire. In the first half of the nineteenth century, frigates grew to 183 feet (56 meters) in length and might have sported upward of sixty cannon. The corvette evolved from the frigate and carried similar rigging. Like the frigate, the corvette was faster and more maneuverable than a ship of the line.

Until the early nineteenth century, warships and merchant vessels were fairly similar. Even in times of peace, protection of cargo required substantial armament, so merchantmen might carry as many as fifty cannon. Large trading ships of Britain, France, and Holland often bore such similarity to men-of-war that serious cases of mistaken identity resulted. Merchant convoys might be attacked by enemy captains who misjudged them as battle fleets; conversely, such convoys might inadver-

Left: In the late 1700s and early 1800s, British and French battle-fleets relied heavily on the seventy-four-gun third-rater. The largest ships in the young American navy of the time were forty-four-gun frigates. Though it appears imposing here, the *U.S.S. Republic* would rank only as a fifth-rater.

Below: When launched in 1850, the *Stag Hound*—built by renowned ship designer Donald McKay—was the largest merchant ship in the world. The very long, narrow design led such vessels to be designated "extreme" clippers.

Left: Painstaking in its detail, a 1665 sketch by an Italian artist illustrates the excess that ship decoration reached during that century. Each country developed its own style, hoping to outdo the others in the proficiency or profusion with which it adorned its ships.

tently avoid attack by appearing to be a gathering of warships. But since the two types were intended for very different purposes, there were significant differences in their construction. Warships required strong decks to support the weight of numerous arms, and they needed a reinforced hull that could survive an enemy barrage with minimal damage. Merchant ships required instead enormous holds for storing cargo.

The art of sailing-ship design culminated in the clipper ship, a class created and built for speed. With wider sails, taller masts, and a long, lean silhouette, the clipper knifed through the water, continually setting new records for velocity. Even the clipper names cried out the swiftness of their nature: *Lightning, Hurricane, Champion of the Seas, Carrier Pigeon, Hornet, Flying Cloud.*

Opposite top: An impressive array of French warships gather in line of file in 1840.

Opposite below: Conquering the open seas with speed and grace, clippers were the ultimate in streamlined sailing-ship design.

Right: Nelson's flagship *Victory*, now preserved in Portsmouth, England, has as its figurehead the coat of arms of the British sovereign.

SAILS, RIGGING, AND OTHER TOOLS OF THE TRADE

The word *ship* has both a general and a precise meaning. All large seagoing vessels are often called ships, but technically a ship has three or more masts—the fore, main, and mizzen—all rigged with square sails. Other vessels broadly categorized as ships include the sloop (a fore-and-aft-rigged, single-masted vessel), the schooner (a vessel with two or more masts and fore-and-aft rigging), the brig (a two-masted square-rigger with headsails

and a spanker sail), and the bark (a vessel with square-rigged fore and main masts and fore-and-aft rigging on the mizzen).

Masts were constructed of pine, and were crossed by the yards, which were usually made from fir and designed to support and spread the sails. Since a single tree was of insufficient height for the masts of a very large ship, such masts were composed of three sections: lower, top, and topgallant mast. Mast design underwent few changes other than the continual endeavor to strengthen the joints between the mast sections and thus to reinforce them against the ravages of weather. By the eighteenth century masts often soared two hundred feet (61 meters) above the water.

The masts and yards were supported by an elaborate maze of rigging to accommodate the ever-growing profusion of sails. Sailing ships generally featured two types of rigging: standing rigging encompassed the ropes, chains, and wires used to support the masts and yards; running rigging served to hoist, lower, and trim the sails. Each mast carried a set of three sails: the main, top (lower and upper), and topgallant sails. The bowsprit, projecting forward from the stem of the ship, gradually became longer to accommodate staysails, spritsails, and jibs—all designed to make the most of wind power. No matter how strong their canvas, sails took quite a beating on the seas and were frequently damaged, requiring prompt repair.

Above: Signal flags often proclaimed a ship's country of origin. In *A King's Ship Dressed with the Colours of Different Nations* (1794), an English ship of the line proudly exhibits the banners of eighty-five maritime cities and countries, each one numbered and identified in the print's border.

Right: Most American clippers had their home port in New York. This nineteenth-century broadside displays the house flags of the city's shipping firms.

Below: A ship's crew tended to consider its figurehead a good luck charm, and often became distraught if it was damaged. This life-size figure of a young woman dates from about 1830–50.

The sail-maker was thus an important part of the crew of every large ship.

At all times, seafarers had to know their position, and the captain's orders had to be obeyed swiftly. Onboard directions refer to the areas of the boat: the bow, or fore, is the front of the boat; the back is known as the aft or stern. The right side came to be known as starboard because the steering board was held on the right side. The left side is port. The weather side is the side from which the wind blows; the sheltered side is leeward.

Finding one's way at sea was sometimes a tall order. Early sailors frequently had to depend on charted landmarks, lighthouses, and buoys. But once removed from the sight of these manmade objects, mariners needed tools to guide them, such as the magnetic compass; the sextant, which measured latitude by showing the angle between two known objects or between the horizon and a celestial body; and the maritime chart, whose accuracy was often questionable, if not downright unreliable. Trusting to visible landmarks for direction presented obvious problems to anyone plying the vastness of the oceans, and the woeful inadequacy of available charts and maps produced many a dangerous miscalculation. An officer sailing with the eighteenth-century French navigator Louis Antoine de Bougainville lamented, "We sail like blind men, having no notion where we are."

Measuring longitude presented great difficulty, since it requires extremely accurate timekeeping, a task at which the primitive shipboard time-measuring instruments of sundial and hourglass were hopelessly inept. So great was the need for navigational improvement that in 1714 the British government offered rewards of thousands of pounds for the invention of an instrument capable of determining longitude. Nearly fifty years later, a carpenter named John Harrison won the prize by producing a relatively accurate chronometer that enabled longitude to be calculated by comparing local time with a fixed standard time. Harrison's timepieces allowed ships that could afford them to navigate with tolerable certainty. It was Harrison's invention that enabled James Cook to carry out his famous explorations.

FIGUREHEADS, CARVINGS, AND SIGNAL FLAGS

Before the seventeenth century, ship decoration was simply painted on hulls and sails. By 1630, decorative sculpture adorned prows and sterns, and after that time figureheads saw widespread use. British ships often bore the heraldic British lion; Danish ships also used a lion or sometimes a swan.

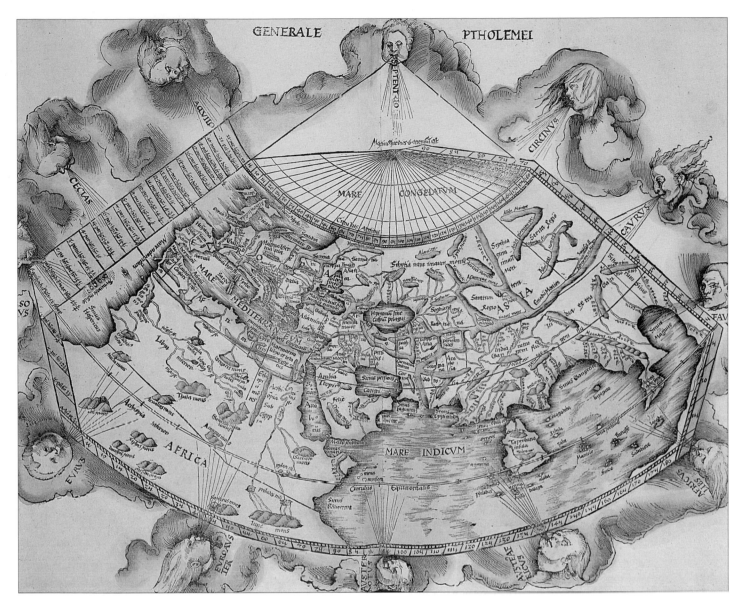

French figureheads were more diverse, often portraying the ship's name or a classical deity. Each country developed its own style, often attempting to outdo the others in the proficiency or elaborateness of its ship ornamentation. Vessels sometimes sported huge escutcheons and emblems, often lavishly gilded. Officers' quarters offered another venue for extravagance, with ornately painted and carved decorations, marquetry, and inlaid paneling. Some of the larger merchant ships were so richly adorned that they began to resemble warships.

The gilding on bow and stern carvings of the seventeenth century later gave way to paint, with black for British ships and blue for French. Around 1780 British vessels appeared the color of natural wood painted with bands of black and red. The French navy featured blue hulls, brown batteries, and red port deadlights. The British Royal Navy, through Admiral Nelson, adopted a band of yellow along each row of ports, edged in white against the black background. A lively black-and-white checkered pattern came into use in the nineteenth century.

The art of the ship carver found its ultimate home on the clippers, where the consummate skill of the carver might be displayed on billetheads, binnacles, transoms, and of course, figureheads. In the words of John W. Griffiths, a leading designer of clipper ships, "The head of a ship stamps an

Above: A fifteenth-century world map, based on Ptolemy's *Geography* of the first century, illustrates the imprecise cartography prevalent until the eighteenth century, when the golden age of maritime exploration at last disclosed the true geography of the earth.

Right: The magnetic compass, used as early as the eleventh century, is still the basic navigational instrument. This example dates from the time of Captain Cook.

impression on the mind in relation to the entire ship." Sadly, as the use of wooden vessels decreased, the craft of the carver began to die out. By the end of the nineteenth century, it had virtually disappeared from the seas.

With its towering masts and huge, billowing sails looming on the horizon long before the hull even came into sight, camouflage at sea was of little use. Since approaching vessels could not help but give considerable advance warning of their approach, they needed a system to identify themselves as friend or foe. Like helmeted medieval warriors requiring elaborate heraldic designs to proclaim their identity and allegiance, ships have for centuries used a language of signal flags to send messages to one another. New information could be passed along by hoisting various combinations of flags on different masts. As well as proudly proclaiming a ship's country of origin—and in the process declaring whether friend or foe to another

Left: The sextant enabled sailors
to determine the angle of celestial
bodies above the horizon.
Coupled with information from a
nautical almanac, the navigator
could thus determine latitude.

passing ship—these flags painted vivid spots of brightly waving colors over
the seas and skies.

THE GREAT EXPLORERS

The golden age of maritime exploration, stretching from about 1740 to
1840, at last disclosed the true nature of the globe. Until that time,
cartography had been considered a secret, a kind of hazy awareness of
coastlines and boundaries that had to be protected from enemy hands. But
gradually exploration evolved from a self-aggrandizing pursuit of new lands
to be conquered into a multinational quest for scientific knowledge.
Mariners began to collaborate with botanists, zoologists, astronomers, and
medical experts, transforming their ships into floating laboratories outfitted
with the latest scientific equipment. The spirit of collaboration even

Right: The compass rose delineated the various wind directions. Such early charts were of limited value until nineteenth-century naval officer Matthew Fontaine Maury compiled sailing directions culled from exhaustive research of ships' logs that enabled him to analyze how winds could be used to best advantage.

Below right: Russian hunters pursue walrus on the icebound Bering Sea. Danish explorer Vitus Bering led a number of Russian expeditions to determine whether Asia and America were joined by land; the strait he discovered in 1728 proved that they were not.

Below: A sailor uses a sextant to help calculate latitude. When measuring the sun's altitude with this device, a navigator was said to be "shooting the sun." First used in 1731, the sextant was much more efficient than its predecessor, the astrolabe.

withstood periods of political turmoil; French officers during the American Revolution, for instance, were under orders to assist the British explorer James Cook if they encountered him.

Many points around the globe were charted during the 1700s. British, French, and Dutch trading companies extensively explored the Indian Ocean during the first half of the century. In 1728 Vitus Jonassen Bering— a Danish navigator in the service of Russia—discovered the strait that now

Left: Over the course of three voyages (1768–79), Captain James Cook's exploration of the Pacific included the Antarctic Circle, New Zealand, Australia, Hawaii, and Alaska, enabling him to chart a substantial portion of the world's largest ocean.

bears his name, proving that water was to be found between Asia and America. The search for the Northwest Passage, through Canada to the Pacific, began early in the century and received renewed impetus when a £20,000 reward was offered to anyone who could discover this passage through Hudson Strait. Although numerous expeditions failed, they did succeed in producing scientific records of great value. Beginning around 1760 the Pacific Ocean was widely explored by teams of scientists and sailors. Led mainly by the French and British, these expeditions covered the sea in all directions from Alaska to the Antarctic and from Chile to Japan. The first scientific explorer of the Antarctic was a French naval officer named Pierre Bouvet, who set out in 1739. But a concerted effort to enter the Antarctic Circle was not made until 1770, when Yves Joseph Kerguelen sailed from France with orders to find the continent due south of Mauritius in the Indian Ocean.

Cartographic achievements during this period were considerable, thanks largely to numerous around-the-world voyages that greatly increased geographic knowledge. The Dutch explorer Jacob Roggeveen embarked on an expedition in 1721 that grew into a circumnavigation of the globe; in the process he discovered Easter Island and evidently sighted part of the Samoan

Archipelago. One of the most important French navigators was Bougainville, who combined military duties with scientific writing during the Seven Years' War, afterward sailing around the world from 1766 to 1769. The British accomplished ten circumnavigations between 1764 and 1790, most notably under the command of Samuel Wallis, who discovered Tahiti in 1767, and Philip Carteret, who discovered the Charlotte Islands, the Gloucester Islands, and Pitcairn Island, and performed valuable surveying work on previously discovered but incompletely charted island groups.

Left: A nineteenth-century
painting, entitled *Captain Cook
Taking Possession of the
Australian Continent on Behalf of
the British Crown*, A.D. 1770,
*under the Name of New South
Wales*, depicts an important event
on Cook's first voyage, on which
he surveyed the whole east coast
of Australia.

JAMES COOK

The most famous explorer of the eighteenth century was James Cook, born
in 1728. After serving as a navigator in the Royal Navy, he was appointed
master of several small craft, and was then occupied in surveying the coast
of Canada and Newfoundland. Respect for his navigational ability led to a
commission as a lieutenant to conduct an expedition to observe the transit
of the planet Venus from Tahiti. He then sailed his ship, the *Endeavour*, in
search of a huge continent reputed to exist in the South Pacific. He

Above: After his brutal regime aboard the *H.M.S. Bounty* instigated a famous mutiny, Captain William Bligh and some of his officers were cast adrift in 1789 by the crew. Astoundingly, with minimal equipment and no charts, Bligh managed to pilot the open craft almost 4,000 miles (6,346 kilometers) to safety.

Right: One of the few explorers to treat the natives with respect, Cook was revered by them in turn. Tragically, during the fray that ensued over a dispute about a stolen boat, he was stabbed to death by a Hawaiian chief.

explored the islands of New Zealand by sea, but the hostility of the inhabitants prevented him from going ashore. He then carefully surveyed the whole east coast of Australia, then known as New Holland. He also named many of the prominent features of the Australian coast, including New South Wales, although he overlooked Sydney Harbor, considering it only a small inlet.

After the enormous success of Cook's first voyage, he was given command of a new expedition, during which, among other accomplishments, he proved that the elusive South Pacific continent did not in fact exist. He also demonstrated the ability of lime juice to conquer scurvy; in a voyage of nearly three years, he lost only one man out of a crew that numbered well over a hundred. On his final voyage, the government ordered him to settle the question of the Northwest Passage by attempting to reach it through the Pacific. Traveling by way of the Cape of Good Hope, he charted several islets in the Cook Archipelago and eventually rediscovered the islands of Hawaii, which had been found by the Spaniards but kept secret. He named the islands after his patron, Lord Sandwich; for many years they were known as the Sandwich Islands. Cook was one of the few captains of his time who encouraged respect for those inhabiting the lands he explored, yet tragically, he met his end at the hands of the Hawaiian Islands' natives in 1779, during an attempt to discover who had stolen one of his boats. But in ten short years he had achieved more than almost any other explorer, mapping new territory, fostering a new spirit of scientific inquiry, and proving that fresh food and fair treatment could go a long way toward improving the lot of the sailor.

Above: Explorers were awed by the Hawaiians' tremendous skill with boats. Here canoeists paddle around the *Blossom,* anchored off Sandwich Bay. "So perfectly masters of themselves in the Water, that it appears their natural Element," declared a contemporary of Cook.

Chapter Two
THE SEAFARING LIFE

How little do the landsmen know of what we sailors feel,
When waves do mount, and wind do blow!
But we have hearts of steel.
No dangers can affright us; no enemy shall flout:
We'll make the Monsieur right us, so toss the can about.
—"The Sailor's Resolution"

In today's world, life of a century or two ago appears proverbially nasty, brutish, and short. Yet without the ships that brought an almost infinite variety of goods from foreign ports and harvested whale oil to produce artificial light, life would have been cruder still. Without the intrepid sailors who made these voyages, none of these amenities would have been possible. And without the sea chantey to ease their labors and unite their efforts, sailors would have found their work even more difficult.

MEN OF THE SEA
For anyone accustomed to the comforts of the late twentieth century, it is difficult to imagine how anyone in earlier times would have endured the extreme hardships of life at sea. The work was hard and unending, discipline was extreme, and flogging was a common occurrence for even the most minor infractions. Living quarters were cramped and filthy. After a storm the ship's interior remained wet for some time, and the crew often slept in their damp clothes to dry them out. Food was ordinarily so atrocious that men preferred to eat in the dark. Provisions were soon filled with insects, butter became rancid, meat quickly turned rotten. And drinking water, stored in wooden casks, immediately became a breeding ground for all manner of bacteria. After two weeks at sea, no one drank more water than was absolutely necessary. To make matters worse, there were always rats and mice on board—sometimes these would even be found floating in the drinking water.

In such conditions sailors were easy prey for a variety of illnesses. Typhoid, typhus, dysentery, malaria, and yellow fever ran rampant at sea,

Opposite: His oilskins donned, his face determined, a nineteenth-century mariner readies himself to face the elements.

Below: The boatswain (sometimes spelled bo'sun because of its pronunciation) was a petty officer in charge of hull maintenance. Whistle at the ready, this Royal Navy boatswain appears about to summon the crew to work.

claiming many lives; it was not uncommon for half of an entire crew to be
lost to disease during a voyage. Scurvy—caused by a lack of Vitamin C—
was a constant threat, since stores of fresh fruits and vegetables were gone
after the first few days. In *Two Years Before the Mast*, Richard Henry
Dana, Jr., recounts the horrors of the disease:

> Besides the natural desire to get home, we had another reason for urging
> the ship on. The scurvy had begun to show itself on board. . . . The
> English lad, Ben, was in a dreadful state, and was daily growing worse.
> His legs swelled and pained him so that he could not walk; his flesh lost
> its elasticity . . . and his gums swelled until he could not open his mouth.

Dana's book, written in 1840 from the journals he kept while at sea,
provides a fascinating account of the life of the common sailor. In his
student days, Dana had shipped aboard the *Pilgrim* on a voyage around
Cape Horn in 1834. He later attended law school; his experiences at sea
and his sympathy for the downtrodden led him to become a sailor's lawyer.
His book eloquently details the harshness of the sailors' lot, the brutality of
his ship's captain, and the absence of recourse open to seamen. "The
captain," he declared, "is lord paramount. He stands no watch, comes and
goes when he pleases, and is accountable to no one, and must be obeyed in
everything without a question, even from his chief officer." Dana also
recounts the rough welcome the crew received from their captain on their
first day out: "'Now, my men, we have begun a long voyage. If we get
along well together, we shall have a comfortable time; if we don't, we shall

Above: The civilized atmosphere
of the midshipman's mess aboard
the *H.M.S. Caesar* in 1856 stands
in stark contrast to the often
appalling conditions under which,
for centuries, the common sailor
was forced to take his meals.

Opposite: *Heavy Weather in the
Channel* perfectly evokes the
formidable task of furling the sails
during a gale. Perched high above
the deck, sailors found themselves
at the mercy of the storm; many
lost their grip and plummeted to
their deaths.

Right: Discipline was often extreme aboard merchant and naval vessel alike, and flogging was a common occurrence for even the most minor infractions.

The Punishments

Right: The very term *press gang* struck fear into the hearts of many men. A favorite source for potential crew members was the local tavern, where some unsuspecting lout in a drunken stupor might be carted off and "pressed" into service to fill the increased need for sailors during wartime.

have hell afloat. All you've got to do is to obey your orders and do your duty like men. . . . If we pull together, you'll find me a clever fellow; if we don't, you'll find me a "bloody" rascal.'"

So why did anyone choose a life at sea? "No man will be a sailor," declared Dr. Samuel Johnson, "who has contrivance enough to get himself into a jail; for being in a ship is being in a jail, with the chance of being drowned. A man in jail has more room, better food and commonly better company." Yet though the sailor's lot might be brutal indeed, it was sometimes preferable to what men faced on land. For some, the sea meant a possibility of escaping even harsher conditions at home. Some were on the run from the law; some were already in jail and welcomed the opportunity of release that shipboard presented. Though there was a ring of truth to Dr. Johnson's pronouncement, jail life was a living hell that any prisoner hoped to escape. During times of crew shortages, it was common

Left: Not even a man on the morning of his wedding day was safe from the infamous press gangs that roamed the towns seeking sailors to increase the fleet.

for crews to be composed largely of convicts. (This condition undoubtedly contributed to the cruel punishments meted out aboard ship in the name of discipline.) And some men had the choice made for them, as the infamous "press gangs" roamed the towns, manning the fleet with those "pressed" into service to fill the increased need for sailors during wartime. In addition, sailors' pay, low as it was, compared favorably with the appalling wages offered by many other occupations. There was even opportunity for advancement. Not all sailors were the oafish fools of stereotype; many were dedicated workers who studied navigation and eventually gained command of their own vessels.

Life aboard ship was not all drudgery and misery. At a time when many people spent their entire lives within the confines of their own village, seafaring offered a chance to see the world. Many crews developed a sense of camaraderie found nowhere else. When all the hard work was done,

Above: Even huge chartered outfits like the East India Company did not give much consideration to speed. It might take over a year to complete the arduous and often storm-filled voyage from England to China and back.

Opposite: Originally built exclusively for the New York to China tea trade, the clipper set such astounding records for speed and efficiency that its use was expanded. This English clipper carries a cargo of wool.

there were entertainments aplenty to be had: musical diversions, games of chance, shore leave in an exotic port, beer and grog to drink. And there was the simple lure of the sea itself. "There is a witchery in the sea," wrote Dana, "its songs and stories, and in the mere sight of a ship and the sailor's dress, especially to a young mind, which has done more to man navies and fill merchantmen than all the press gangs of Europe."

TRADE ROUTES AND MERCHANTMEN

The major European nations did not completely appreciate the economic importance of the sea until the seventeenth century. Prior to that time the oceans provided an opportunity for colonial expansion and served as a proving ground for naval supremacy. But the establishment of far-flung colonies magnified the possibilities for international trade and helped to secure markets for previously unknown products such as coffee, sugar, and exotic spices. As America, Asia, and Africa continually supplied the mother

THE WHALE FISHERY "LAYING ON,"

THE AMERICAN REVOLUTION

The American Revolution had a profound effect on merchant shipping throughout the world. Until then the outfitting of ships for maritime trade had mostly been a small-scale, family business. Many European ship owners had only one vessel and sometimes even commanded it themselves. Even huge chartered outfits like the East India Company did not give much consideration to speed; a round-trip England-to-China voyage could take more than a year, and a convoy bound for Ceylon and India might take up to a year and a half. But in the newly formed United States, the quest for larger and faster ships inevitably led to more expensive vessels whose construction and operation required the considerable financial backing of merchant trading companies.

In a market dominated by the long-established maritime powers of Europe, Americans had to create a niche for themselves. They did it by getting in on the China trade, since the port of Canton was virtually the only one not controlled by the monopolies held by chartered companies granted exclusive trading rights. They also built a new type of ship, the clipper, whose reign over the seas was short-lived but dramatic. Originating around the 1840s and fading from use only a few decades

Above: A Currier & Ives print of 1852 shows the "laying on," where, harpoons at the ready, whalers approach the creature in preparation for the kill. They must row close enough for the weapon to find its mark, but not so near that the thrashes of the maddened whale will threaten their tiny boats.

Opposite: The heyday of whaling was the nineteenth century, but the practice actually dates back to prehistoric times. The British and Dutch led the industry in early modern times, as this seventeenth-century Dutch print illustrates; by that time Holland boasted almost two hundred whalers.

Above: The rich concentration of plankton in Greenland waters made it a bountiful whaling ground. Here, in one dramatic and alarming moment, a Greenland whale upends a whaleboat with a whip of its tail, hurling the terrified crew into the air.

later, clippers were originally built exclusively for the New York to China tea trade, when speed of delivery became all-important in the race to deliver the freshest tea.

For the famous clipper ships, "sailing day" was a grand occasion that attracted huge crowds. All the great ships had enthusiastic followers who flocked to the wharves to wish them swift and successful voyages, and filled the docks with cheers to welcome them home. The clippers returned from China laden with tea, yet stowed among the chests in the hold were many other enticements, leading to an insatiable hunger for *chinoiserie:* handmade Oriental articles such as porcelains, lacquered furnishings, carved ivory objects, colorful silks, and painted fans. What began as means to reap enormous profits from the sale of a popular beverage soon reached dizzying heights of commercial success.

THE WHALERS

Pitting humankind against the forces of nature was a favorite nineteenth-century theme. And what greater embodiment of man triumphing over the forces of evil than the thrill of whaling, of defeating a beast described by *Moby Dick*'s Captain Ahab as "the gliding great demon of the seas of life." By mid-century—the heyday of the industry—whaling had become a serious business, one of the first major industries of North America and worth nearly ten million dollars a year. Before the advent of kerosene, whales were a principal source of oil for artificial light, and the oil was also used in making soap and candles. Whalebone—which is actually the hard plate from the roof of the whale's mouth—was eagerly sought in the realm of fashion, to produce stays for the ubiquitous corset and as ribbing for

umbrellas. Ambergris, a rare substance sometimes found in the whale's intestines, was highly prized as a fixative for perfume and was worth much more than its weight in gold.

After decades of fierce international competition, New England emerged as the dominant force in this primarily American industry. Whale products were frequently sold in England, whose economy was stronger than that of the still-struggling states. The foremost whaling port of the late eighteenth and early nineteenth centuries was Nantucket. After carrying the goods to London, the vessels would return with European products for the home market. (In 1773, a Nantucket whaler sailed into Boston Harbor along with a Boston merchant ship, filled with return cargoes of English tea, the very cargo thrown overboard by angry colonists in the infamous Boston Tea Party.) But Nantucket's near-monopoly in whaling was soon eclipsed by another Massachusetts location—New Bedford, which for many years was the whaling capital of the world. By the 1850s, four-fifths of all American whaleships—more than half the fleet of the entire world—sailed out of this tiny town.

Whaling was a hard and dangerous trade. The excursions were grueling, often lasting two or three years. All seagoing vessels were subject to the perils of severe weather and all crews had to endure the routine toils of shipboard life accompanied by harsh treatment and appalling food. But the whaler sailed with the added threat of a life-or-death battle with a wounded fifty-ton creature thrashing madly about. While the ship owners and captains often became very rich, the whalemen themselves could barely earn a living. In lieu of wages the men oftentimes received a share in the profits of the voyage. But by the time all expenses were deducted and the

Above: Once the whale was hauled to the larger ship, the head was cut off and brought aboard. The men climbed into the head to retrieve the blubber or, in this case, the spermaceti that would be used in making soap, cosmetics, ointments, and candles.

Left: To compound the already excessive hazards of whaling—rough seas and the potentially fatal gyrations of a wounded fifty-ton animal—these whalers must contend with the additional dangers of navigating a polar sea as they steer perilously close to the jagged ice.

Above: Though it looks as if the ship is on fire, the flames and thick smoke actually result from the boiling of whale blubber to render it into the valuable oil that was an important component of the era's artificial lighting.

profits divided, there was precious little left to take home. Yet to some this was preferable to the life they had left behind, since whaling crews were sometimes culled from jails or were deserters from the British Navy who remained safe as long as they were on an American ship.

After many uneventful days at sea, the monotony would be broken by cries of "Blo-ow! Blo-ow!" Once sighted, the whale was pursued in small boats launched from the larger ship, which waited at a distance. When the crew rowed within striking distance, the harpooneer fired the weapon. If the harpoon struck its mark, it then fell to the mate to lance and kill the whale. This job required great proficiency, since even a mortally wounded whale could exert enormous force, often smashing a small whaleboat to bits. After the whale finally died, it was hauled to the larger ship and hoisted alongside. The whaling crew then had to perform the unenviable tasks of "cutting in" and "stowing away." The head was cut off and brought aboard; to retrieve blubber that would be rendered into valuable oil the men had to climb into the head and wade waist-deep in the loose fat. As the blubber was boiled, thick clouds of smoke arose, accompanied by an unbearable stench. Work progressed unceasingly until the fifteen tons or more of oil were safely stowed.

Between whale sightings came endless days at sea. To relieve the debilitating boredom, whalemen filled their free hours by carving whalebone and teeth into trinkets and household objects. Known as scrimshaw, this skill evolved into a highly collectible art in the hands of the most talented scrimshanders. The carving tool was often a simple jackknife; if further decoration was desired, a sail needle was used to inscribe a design that was then rubbed with a mixture of oil and lampblack. Scrimshanders produced a seemingly endless array of popular items, including clothespins, bird cages, walking stick handles, eggcups, butter knives, rolling pins, and jagging wheels, used to crimp the edges of a piecrust. One of the most demanding items made by scrimshanders was the swift, an instrument used for winding yarn; its construction required the manipulation of dozens of whalebone strips into an expandable framework fastened with ribbons and metal pivots. Though the era of the whaler is long gone, the creations of the scrimshander survive as a reminder of this once crucial industry.

SEA CHANTEYS AND WORK SONGS

According to some historians of music, the primitive work chant was the ancestor of all song. It sprang to life whenever people had to do hard labor with only their hands and a spirit of cooperation to aid in the work. The word *chantey*—derived from the French *chanter,* meaning to sing—probably did not come into popular usage until the nineteenth century, but the practice of singing such songs at sea has a much longer history. A fifteenth-century Venetian friar was the first to write about chanteying: "There are others who sing when work is going on, because work at sea is very heavy, and is only carried on by a concert between one who sings out orders and the laborers who sing in response."

Work songs were common to many professions; they were sung by farmers and cowboys, loggers and railroaders, pioneers and slaves. Sea chanteys comprise one of the largest groups of work songs. According to Alan Lomax, a renowned authority on folk songs, "The chanteys arose among the despised common seamen, as they fought the drag of line and anchor and bawled out whatever wild cries, oaths, and barbarities would help them in their struggle with wind and sea."

Weighing anchor and hoisting sails required strength, determination, and above all, team effort. To set the rhythm of the work and keep the concerted effort flowing, the chanteyman would begin the song, sometimes composing it as he went along, always setting it to a traditional tune. Then the gang would join in on the chorus, the lilt of the chant lending cadence to the job. With

Above: This whalebone ship model was made by a French naval prisoner during the Napoleonic Wars. Despite the astonishing intricacy of detail, such work is not unique—many models of ships and other objects were created by prisoners at that time.

Left: To fill their free hours at sea, sailors carved whalebone and teeth into a variety of trinkets and household objects. A mixture of oil and lampblack was rubbed over the item to highlight the inscribed design, as in this intricate scrimshaw depicting a man's farewell to his family.

Right: The object that perhaps most taxed the skill of the scrimshander was the swift, a complex instrument for winding yarn. Its delicate construction required dozens of whalebone strips to be manipulated into an expandable framework, fastened with ribbons and metal pivots.

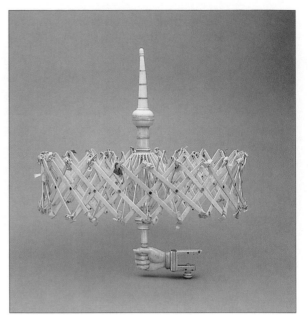

each pull on the rope another line was sung; each answering pull dictated a corresponding reply in song. Capstan and windlass chanteys, used in "catting" or weighing anchor or hoisting sails, display the greatest variations and loveliest melodies of all sea songs. The halyard or long-drag chantey was used for work at topsails and topgallant sails. Sheet, tack, and bowline songs—also known as short-drag chanteys—were probably the oldest form of sailors' work song. They were sung during quick jobs, when hauling sheets aft and fastening bowlines.

By the eighteenth century, though chanteying remained in favor on smaller English ships, it had been dispensed with aboard larger vessels. Naval practice did not allow it; servicemen had to work in silence and obey the boatswain's whistle. The quasi-military discipline of the heavily armed merchant ships also discouraged work songs. But as the American merchant marine rose around 1815, the chantey returned in full force. Once the American packets and clippers had begun their regular runs, these

Below: Scrimshaw decorates this ditty box, whose oval sides are made of baleen (the flexible whale membrane also known as whalebone). A ditty box was a container in which the sailor kept personal effects or sewing implements.

Above: The great age of sail lasted well into the nineteenth century, but the coming primacy of steam power is foretold as a small steamboat glides alongside the *U.S.S. Columbia.*

songs again proved their usefulness: a small crew handling a large, fast ship plainly needed the chantey to get the work done. The tradition grew stronger still in the 1860s with the return of the British merchant marine's predominance.

Beyond the service of setting the laborer's pace, the sea chantey provided just about the only means the common seaman had of voicing his grievances. Countless songs lament the harshness of the sailor's life: the rough conditions on board, the dread of a storm at sea, the threat of pirates, the discrimination the sailor faced when ashore, the brutality of a sadistic first mate, or the yearning to return home from a long voyage. Songs also abound on the theme of whaling, lyrically describing the thrill and terror of catching the whale, and the horrors of processing it.

Yet there are also many songs of jubilation, celebrating the excitement of preparing to set sail, the spirit of togetherness among the crew, the anticipation of a homeward-bound journey, and of course, the joys of drinking and of rediscovering the companionship of women. The time-honored tradition of the chantey exhibits a rollicking energy found nowhere else.

Right: The awesome power of wind and sea is unleashed in *A First-Rate Man-of-War Driving on a Reef of Rocks, Foundering in a Gale*. To classify their degree of force, winds were divided into twelve types, ranging from light air to moderate gale to hurricane.

sailors plummeted to the deck or plunged into the raging sea.

The loss of a man quelled the spirits of even the rowdiest crew. Confined to close quarters, working side by side for months or even years, sailors felt the absence of one of their number acutely. As Dana described it, "Death is at all times solemn, but never so much so as at sea. A man dies on shore—his body remains with his friends . . . but when a man falls overboard at sea and is lost, there is a suddenness in the event, and a difficulty in realizing it, which give to it an air of awful mystery."

GREAT MARITIME BATTLES

Throughout the eighteenth century, the rival between England and France was essentially a struggle for mastery of the seas. The supremacy of the British Navy was the principal reason for France's loss of its colonies in North America. Though Great Britain signed a peace treaty with her victorious American colonies in 1783, fighting continued. Locked in a ferocious struggle with Napoleon, the Royal Navy was seizing American ships, both to prevent the possibility of cargo falling into French hands and to impress American sailors into British service. In 1812, war was officially declared. To Britain's astonishment, America—with a navy only sixteen ships strong—was victorious at sea for the first year. But the tide had turned by the end of the following year.

Twenty miles (32 kilometers) west of Cape Trafalgar on the southern point of Spain a force of twenty-seven warships under the general command of Admiral Viscount Horatio Nelson met and engaged Admiral Pierre Charles Villeneuve's heavily armed fleet of thirty-three Spanish and French vessels (known as the Combined Fleet) on October 21, 1805. Though the sides were closely matched, Admiral Nelson's imaginative and skillful tactics enabled the Royal Navy to carry the day. The conventional attack pattern called for the attacking line of ships to lay close alongside

Opposite top: Arthur William Devis' *The Death of* Nelson captures the great admiral's final moments. After being shot he was carried below, draped in sailcloth at his own request so his men would not lose their spirit upon seeing their commander mortally wounded.

Opposite below: To cheer his fleet just before battle, Admiral Nelson had his signal lieutenant send a now-famous message, using the sophisticated Naval flag code that the British had recently perfected.

Left: When war was declared in 1812, the fledgling American navy amazed its British foes by proving victorious the first year. Here the frigate *United States* captures the British frigate *Macedonian*.

Right: In retaliation against the colonists for having sunk the *Victory* (the namesake of Nelson's famous flagship), the Royal Navy destroys an American warship in 1779.

Below: A naval review at Portsmouth, England, in 1814 honors the czar of Russia and the king of Prussia. In addition to paying tribute to important dignitaries, a display such as this enabled the British king to impress other nations with the splendor and power of the Royal Navy.

the defenders, ship to ship, and attempt to break through the defensive line individually by furious broadsiding. Eschewing these tactics, Nelson divided his own force into two lines and intersected Villeneuve's line in two separate places. This enabled each of the two British divisions to attack one-third of the enemy's ships, while the remaining third would be faced with the difficult maneuver of traveling astern to assist those under attack.

This ingenious plan caught the French and Spanish off guard. Nelson, on board the 104-gun *Victory,* and his second in command, Vice Admiral Cuthbert Collingwood, aboard the 100-gun *Royal Sovereign,* each led half the British forces in two spearhead attacks and threw the Combined Fleet in disarray. After a grueling battle lasting over four hours, the French and Spanish ships were on fire, sinking, or otherwise disabled. The British suffered heavy losses themselves, most significantly Lord Nelson himself, who was felled by a sniper's bullet as he stood on the *Victory*'s top deck. Thus the commander of England's great naval victories at Copenhagen and the Nile met his end during the battle that proved British naval superiority in Europe. Through its victory at Trafalgar, the Royal Navy ensured the ultimate defeat of Napoleon, who was left to wage war on the Continent without the ability to blockade opposing ports or interfere with nautical trade routes.

Above: The *H.M.S. Bulldog* bombards Bomarsund in the Crimea. The neatly dressed officers and crew belie the fact that the Crimean War (1854–56) was a terribly bloody—though inconclusive—campaign, waged by Britain and France against Russia's attempts at further westward expansion.

Previous page below: : When a storm threatened, sails had to be furled immediately to preserve them from the ravages of the wind. The clipper ship *Comet* of New York seems not to have attended to this task in time—one of its sails has been torn away completely.

Sea battles also played an important role in the War of 1812. The most celebrated American ship during that campaign was the frigate *Constitution,* whose oaken ribs were spaced so closely together beneath the outer timbers that cannonballs bounced off the hull, earning it the nickname "Old Ironsides." At no time was this quality better demonstrated than in the *Constitution*'s engagement with the English frigate *Guerriere,* about two hundred miles (322 kilometers) off the coast of Nova Scotia. As the *Constitution* approached, the *Guerriere* greeted it with a constant barrage. But the American captain, Isaac Hull—confident in his assessment that the enemy's gunnery possessed only moderate accuracy and that his own ship could withstand heavy fire—did not give the order to fire until his ship had come within extremely close range, about twenty-five yards (23

meters) from the enemy. Then the American gunners let loose at his command. The *Guerriere* was instantly splintered and all three masts were soon shot away. Despite the *Guerriere*'s heavy fire at such close range, the *Constitution*'s "iron" sides had protected the crew so well that only seven American sailors were killed and seven wounded.

THE AGE OF STEAM

With the coming dominance of steam propulsion, the change in armaments after 1850, and the increasing efficiency of vessels built of iron and steel, the wooden sailing ship gradually lost its authority over the high seas. But its centuries-long reign had been grand indeed, and its power over the imagination still holds sway.

$\mathscr{I}$NDEX

Page numbers in **boldface** refer to photo captions.

Admiral of the Fleet, **15**
Adventure Galley, **62**
Alarm, **68**
Alaska, 29, **29**
ambergris, 49
American colonies, 40, 63
  Boston Tea Party, **43**, 49
  naval battles with Britain, 73, **76**
American Revolution, 28, 47–48
Antartic Circle, 29, **29**, 64
around-the-world voyages, 29–30
Australia, 29, 31, 33, **67**

Bahamas, 63
barks, **6**, 23, **43**
battles at sea, 73–79, **76**
  line formation, 12, **13**, 73–77
  Trafalgar, **73**, 73–7
  War of 1812, 73, **75**, 78–79
Beal, Reynolds, **58**
  Trade Winds, **79**
Bering, Vitus Jonassen, 28, **28**–29
Bering Strait, **28**, 28–29
Blackbeard (Edward Teach), **5**, 63
Bligh, Capt. William, **32**
Blossom, **33**
"Blue China" Craze, The, **45**
boats, 5–8
  Hawaiians' skill with, **33**
  use in whaling, **47**, **48**, 52
boatswains, **35**, 54
Boston Tea Party, **43**, 49
Bougainville, Louis Antoine de, 24, 30
Bouvet, Pierre, 29
bowsprit, 23
Bradley, Milton, **57**
brig, 22–23
Britain
  and American colonies, **43**, 73
  Crimean War, **77**
  maritime rivalries, 11, **43**, 73
  merchant marine, 55
  U.S. trade with, 49
  voyages of exploration, 28, 29, 31–33
  War of 1812, 73, **75**, 78–79
  whaling industry, 47
British East India Company, 40, 43–45, **47**, 64
British Royal Navy, 31, **35**, 63, 73, **73**
  battle of Trafalgar, **73**, 73–77
  colors, 25
  deserters, 52, 58
  engagements with American ships, 73, **76**
  fleet organization, **15**
  naval review at Portsmouth, **76**
British ships
  clipper, **40**
  colors, 25
  Dutton near shipwreck, **9**
  figureheads, **22**, 24
  first-raters, 11
  frigates, 18
  hulls of, 15
  merchant ships, 18
  ships of the line, 18, **23**
  third-raters, 13, **19**
Burns, Robert, 18

Canada, 29, 31
Canton, China, 47
Cape Horn passage, 37, 63–67, **65**, **67**
Cape of Good Hope passage, 33, **44**, **59**
Captain Cook Taking Possession of the Australian Continent, **31**
Carteret, Philip, 30
cartography, **25**, **29**, 29–30
chanteys, 53–55
Charlotte Islands, 30
China trade, 40, 43, 47, 48
Chinese junks, **64**
Chinese porcelain, **45**
chinoiserie, **45**, 48
circumnavigation of globe, 29–30
clipper ships, **15**, 21, **21**, 40, 47–48, 54–55, **57**, 64
  Cape Horn passage, **67**, 67
  China trade, 40, **45**
  decoration, 25–26
  Comet in storm, **78**

Cutty Sark, **15**, 18
"extreme," **19**
U.S., **24**, 47–48
vulnerability to fire, **67**
Collingwood, Vice Admiral Cuthbert, 77
Combined Fleet, 73–77
Comet, **78**
compass rose, **28**
Conrad, Joseph, 57
Constitution ("Old Ironsides"), 78–79
convoys, 18–21, **43**, 47
Cook, Capt. James, **15**, 24, **26**, 28, **29**, 31–33, **31**, **32**, **33**, 65–67
Cook Archipelago, 33
Cornwall, England, 67
corvette, 18
Crimean War, **77**
Currier & Ives prints, **47**, **67**
Cutty Sark, **15**, 18

Dana, Richard Henry, Jr., 37–38, 40, 69, 73
Danish figureheads, 24
Darling, James and Grace, **69**
Dawson, Henry, *Guardship Saluting*, **15**
Death of Nelson, The (Devis), **73**
Devis, **Arthur** William, *The Death of Nelson*, **73**
Drake Passage, 64
Dutton, **9**

East African, **43**
Easter Island, 29
East Indiaman, 43
Egyptian vessels, 8
Emily, **69**
Endeavor, **15**, 31
exploration, **15**, **25**, 27–33

fifth-rater, **19**
figureheads, **9**, **22**, 24, 24–25
first-raters, 11, **70**
First-Rate Man-of-War Driving on a Reef of Rocks, A, **70**
Flying Cloud, 11, 21, 67
Flying Dutchman, **59**
France, **43**, **77**
  maritime rivalries, **43**, 73
  voyages of exploration, 28, 29, 30
French Navy, **5**, 25, 73–77
French ships
  figureheads, 25
  frigates, 18
  hulls of, 15
  merchant vessels, 18
  third-raters, 13, **19**
  warships, **21**
frigates, 15–18

galley (trireme), 9
George III, king of England, **43**
ghost ships, **59**
Gloucester Islands, 30
Golden Light, **67**
Grant, Ulysses S., **9**
Greek vessels, 8, 9
Greenland, 48
Griffiths, John W., 25–26
Guardship Saluting (Dawson), **15**
Guerriere, 78–79
gunneries and cannon, **5**, 11–13, **13**, 15, 18, **19**

Hawaiian Islands, **29**, **32**, 33, **33**
Heavy Weather on the Channel, **37**
H.M.S. *Bounty*, **32**
H.M.S. *Bulldog*, **37**
H.M.S. *Caesar*, **37**
H.M.S. *Topaz*, **65**
Holbein, Hans, *Ship with Armed Men*, **11**
Holland, **11**, 18, 28, **43**, 47
Huggins, William, **73**
Hull, Isaac, 78
hulls, 15, **15**, 21, 35

Indian Ocean exploration, 28, 29
India trade, **43**, 47

Kerguelen, Yves Joseph, 29
Kidd, Capt. William, 59–63, **62**
King's Ship Dressed with the Colours of Different Nations, A, **23**

La Montagne, **13**
latitude measurement, 24, **27**, **28**
longboat, 9
longitude measurement, 24

Macedonia, **75**
McKay, Donald, **19**, 67
magnetic compass, 24, **26**
mail transport, **43**, **43**
maps and charts, 24, **25**, **28**, **29**, 29–30, 67
"Mariners of Britain, The," 57
masts, 22, 23
Maury, Matthew Fontaine, **28**, 67
Maynard, Lt. Robert, 63
Melville, Herman, 57
men-of-war, **13**, **15**, 18, **70**; *see also* warships
merchant ships, 18-21, 40–43, 47
  armed, **11**, 13, 18, **64**
  Cape Horn passage, 67
  clippers as, **19**, 47–48, **40**
  convoys of, 18-21, **43**, 47
  discipline aboard, **38**, 54, 58
  frigates, 15–18
  out of New York, **24**, **44**
  piracy of, **64**
Moby Dick (Melville), 48
Molly, **6**
Mort de Virginie, La (Vernet), **59**

Nantucket, 49
Napoleonic Wars, **5**, 53, 73, 77
navigation tools, 24
  charts and maps, 24, **28**, 67
  Harrison chronometer, 24
  magnetic compass, 24, **26**
  sextant, 24, **27**, **28**
navigators, *see* Bougainville; Cook
Nelson, Adm. Viscount Horatio, 22, 25, 73–77, **73**, **76**
New Bedford, Massachusetts, 49, **58**
New England, 49
Newfoundland, 31
New South Wales, **31**, 33
New York, **24**, 40, **44**, **45**, 48, 78
New Zealand, **29**, 33
Northwest Passage, search for, 29, 33

oar-powered boats, 9
Odysseus, 57
Orpheus, **43**

Pacific Ocean exploration, 29, **29**, 31–33, **31**
packets, **43**, 54
passenger transport, **43**, **44**, 45
Patina, **58**
Phoenician vessels, 8
Pilgrim, 37
pirates, **5**, 18, 57-63, **57**, **62**, **63**, **64**
Pitcairn Island, 30
Portsmouth, England, 22, **43**, **76**
press gangs, **38**, **39**, **39**, 40
Ptolemy, **25**
Pyle, Howard, **57**, **62**

Red Jacket, **67**
Resolution, **11**
rigging, 23
Roggeveen, Jacob, 29–30
Roman vessels, 8, 9
"Round the World" board game, **57**
Royal Sovereign, 77
Russia, **28**, 28–29, **76**, 77

sail boats, 8
sail-maker, 24
sailors, **11**, 35–40
  death at sea, 73
  discipline and punishment of, **35**, **38**, **39**, 54, 58
  earnings of, 8, **39**, 49–52, 58
  illnesses of, 35–37
  impressment of, **38**, **39**, **39**, 40
  on pirate ships, 58
  during storms, **37**, 69–73
  whalemen, **47**, 49–52, **49**
  "Sailor's Alphabet, The," **5**
  "Sailor's Resolution, The," 35
sails, 23–24
  early use of, 8-9
  furling of, before storms, **37**, 69, 78

rigging for, 23
square, 8, 22
work songs associated with hoisting, 53–54
Samoan Archipelago, 29–30
Sandwich Islands, 33; *see also* Hawaiian Islands
schooner, 22
Schouten, Capt. Willem, 63
Scilly Isles, 67
scrimshaw and scrimshanders, 52–53, **54**
scurvy, 33, 37
sea chanteys, 53–55
Seven Years' War, 30
sextants, 24, **27**, **28**
ship carvers, 25–26
ship models, **53**
ships, 22
  classes of, 11–13
  design of, 11–21, **15**
  food aboard, 35, 37, 43
  gunneries and cannon, **5**, 11–13, **13**, 15–18
  ornamentation and decoration, **12**, 21, 24–26
  predecessor vessels, 5–9
  signal flags, **23**, 24, 26–27, 73
  steering gear, 13–15
  superseded by steam-propelled vessels, 9, 79
  terminology for directions on, 24
  timekeeping aboard, 24
  vessels broadly categorized as, 22-23
ships of the line, 11, **13**, 18, **23**
Ship with Armed Men (Holbein), **11**
shipwrecks, 9, **59**, 67-73, **67**, **68**, **69**, **70**
signal flags, **23**, 24, 26–27, 59, 73
sloop, 22
Sovereign of the Seas, **12**
Spain, 33, **43**, 73–77
Spithead, England, ship arriving at, **15**
Stag Hound, **19**
steam-propelled vessels, 9, **55**, 79
steering gear, 13-15
storms at sea, **37**, 64–65, **65**, 67–73, **67**, **68**, **69**, **70**
swift, 53, **54**
Sydney Harbor, 33

Tahiti, 30, 31
Teach, Edward (Blackbeard), 63
tea trade, 40, **43**, **45**, 48, 49
third-raters, 13, **19**
Tierra del Fuego, 65–67
trade routes, 40-43
Trade Winds (Beal), **79**
Trafalgar, battle of, **73**, 73–77
trireme (galley), 9
Turner, J. M. W., 37
Two Years before the Mast (Dana), 37

United States, **75**
United States
  China trade, **45**, 47–48
  clipper ships, **24**, 47–48
  naval ships, 13, **19**, 73
  merchant marine, 54
  in War of 1812, 73, **75**, 78–79
  whaling industry, 49, **58**
U.S.S. Columbia, **55**
U.S.S. Republic, **19**

Vernet, Joseph, *La Mort de Virginie*, **59**
Victory, 22, **76**, 77
Viking vessels, 8, 9
Villeneuve, Adm. Pierre Charles, 73–77

walking the plank, **57**
Wallis, Samuel, 30
War of 1812, 73, **75**, 78–79
warships, **12**, **15**, 21, **21**, **70**, **76**
  as escorts, 43
  ratings, 11-13
  ships of the line, **11**, **13**, 18, **23**
whaling, **47**, 48-53, **51**, **52**, 55, **58**
winds, **70**, **79**
  around Cape Horn, 64–65
  charting direction of, **28**, 67
work songs, 53–55

yards, 8, 23